Celebrations for Special Days and Occasions

Celebrations
for Special Days
and Occasions

by Jack W. Lundin

Illustrated by
Josephine Mulhearn

1817

HARPER & ROW PUBLISHERS

New York, Evanston, San Francisco, London

To my wife Marti and daughter Julie,
and for the special days and many occasions
we celebrate together

Contents

IV. SEASONAL RECOGNITION

V. THE HOLY SUPPER

Foreword

A great deal of listening has gone into this little book. Each of the chapters, most of which have been tested out in families, has a kind of felt-reasoning behind it. Let me tell you about it.

It all started one Sunday morning in a worship service I was conducting. Before the sermon there is usually a hymn, and before the hymn there may be "reason" to make certain announcements. All such announcements of weekly events are printed in the bulletin, but there has grown, especially among Protestants, a peculiar habit of reciting in front of the congregation those same dates and times dictated to the church secretary just a few days earlier. And so it was to be on that Sunday. The announcements pretty well split up the various members of the family, each to an evening, and each—by age, sex, or interest—to be invited to spend that particular time doing something related to Christianity with people like oneself. On that specific Sunday there wasn't even a Family Night to rescue me! I realized then that the church is not really organized in ways which would give evidence of some compassionate understanding of the needs of the family. By the way, my sermon that Sunday was on the subject of family unity. I remember making it through the first five or six sentences before apologizing for daring to say one thing and do another. From that day on I tried to listen honestly to what families are saying. The chapters you will find in this book are reflections on that process.

Listening also requires one to hear and be aware of rumblings outside the family. Theodore Roszak's book has introduced us to the counter-culture as particularly, but by no means entirely, represented in the young. But then, many of us have sensed the spirit and verve of the counter-culture in our own children. They are smarter, more insistent in their examination of usable values, unwilling to be "conned" by anybody, and generally, despite all the publicity which has them challenging systems, are the "Yes! Generation"; affirming life and willing to love and to risk. And best of all, again running against popular grain, they are the youth in search of family. We see the family going beyond the biological relation into support groupings, whether communes or simply the ordinary peer group dependency where secrets are shared and dreams spun without criticism. Shouldn't this happen in the family? And if we Christians talk about reconciliation and celebrating Life as a gift from God in His Son, then cannot such an exciting invitation into living become again the common property of the Chrstian family?

My thanks to those who encouraged me; to the people of the experimental congregation I currently serve, the Community of Christ the Servant. They have been willing to risk making mistakes along with the hope of finding fresh patterns for family communication. The possibility of becoming open toward each other, in family and congregation, has led to much happiness and trust.

I also wish to thank two friends whose support of our experiment means a great deal: Martin Marty and David Granskou.

And just where would any author be without those who provide daily support, love, momentous interruptions, hurts

which need immediate attention, love waiting to be shared!
To my wife Marti and our daughter Julie Ann, my thanks,
love, and gratitude for allowing me to be husband and father
in a rather special pastoral way.

JACK W. LUNDIN

I. The Family Cup of Blessing

1. The Story of the Cup

Religious history tells the fascinating story of how the most common drinking utensil became invested with unusual symbolic power. We suggest a Cup, homemade or purchased, for most all of the family celebrations.

Throughout man's history the Cup has been used in religious ceremony as the symbol of unity for community, family, tribe, and it has long held prominence in special ceremonies such as weddings (Eastern Orthodox especially), and as the chalice or common Cup passed among the faithful during the Eucharist. The Cup in Jewish history is singularly important. As an example: Nehemiah was honored and trusted as King Artaxerxes' "taster" (Neh. 1:11), and was called a Cupbearer. Remember the story of Benjamin and the cup hidden in his sack, with the meaning it had for him and his father (Gen. 44:2 ff.)? The symbolism of the Cup runs through the pages of the Old and New Testaments. In one place it is the Cup of happiness which overflows (Ps. 23:5), and in another it represents the bitterness of man's situation (Ps. 11:6). The Cup of Salvation in Psalm 116 is a familiar theme, as is the New Testament use of that same theme in the person of the Messiah. Jesus spoke of the Cup of impending suffering (Matt. 26:39) and prayed that He might not drink of it. Again he used the theme of the Cup as He questioned His followers concerning their willingness to experience His suffering (Matt. 20:22).

Most significant for the Christian, however, is the identity which the Cup has in the Eucharist: the truly celebrational Cup of Christ's blood, the Cup turned into chalice, the common made unusually rich and invested with symbolism which encompasses the whole grace of God and His love for man. The word Eucharist carries with it not only the theme of the Supper between Jesus Christ and His followers, but also the ideas of mutual sharing and of joyous thanksgiving!

For our purposes the Cup becomes the symbol for family celebration, for insight into each other's lives, and for reconciliation. It is suggested that everyone in the family choose the Cup in order that it *belong* to all. (See "A Dedication of the Family Cup.")

Families know the enormous pressures in our rapidly changing society. We all need some bond to help us maintain a sense of common destiny and a fresh hope for our future. The Cup can become a tangible symbol, filled with the juices reflective of and made a part of the family tradition.

So let the Cup enhance conversation; welcome the stranger; share hopes as well as fears. Let the Cup become to your family what it has become in many a religious home, especially those of the Jewish faith. At Passover the youngest son is chosen to ask the questions concerning the festival. Then the head of the family raises the Cup of Blessing in a beautiful and sensitive salute to the remembrances of a grace which has already provided the family with its oneness in God.

Make the Cup your Family Cup of Blessing.

2. Dedication of the Family Cup

You'll want to take time to get just the right cup to symbolize your own family's style of life. Maybe you'll want to buy a basic cup and then add drawn symbols or paste-ons. After you have purchased and/or created what you want, then dedicate it together as a family. The following is suggested.

Leader (*with cup unfilled*): Asking the blessings of God for us all, we come together to dedicate this cup.

Family: May it symbolize the deep emotions of our life together.

Leader: May it represent a shared love which may grow, by Your grace, every day.

Family: May it be a sign of the trust we have in You as

our God and a willingness to share values, feelings, and hopes with each other.

Leader: Blessed be this Cup of Blessing. May we use it in times of sorrows and joys in order that our sense of mutual family love may continually know Your rich grace.

Family: So be it.

Now fill the Cup and share it all around. A napkin may be passed with the chalice.

II. Holiday Celebrations

3. Advent Secrets

An old European custom has the days of Advent—the four weeks before Christmas—become filled with surprises for the whole family. Here's how it goes. Write the names of every member of the family on a small piece of paper and drop them into a box. For the fun of it mark the box "Advent Secrets." Gather the family to draw names, making sure you don't draw your own. During the days of Advent, plan out secret acts of love toward the person whose name you've drawn. Here's a liturgy to get it all started.

Leader (*with the family together and the box filled with names*): Remembering how the prophets provided an ancient people with hints that God would love and save them, we, as a family, imitate that theme in Advent through acts of love toward each other done in secret.

Family: We plan our acts of love because we are a family.

Leader: We do it for fun.

Family: We do it with thanks to God for giving us both imagination and a sense of family playfulness.

4. Christmas—Gifts Seen and Unseen

Christmas means belonging! To God, of course, and to each other! There comes a time—a season for the Christian—to realize that there is absolutely no fickleness about His acceptance of us. There are embarrassing hints that we know this to be true. Even all-out war usually calls a truce. The Prince of Peace invades our separation-from-each-other routine and once again, we belong! For His own reasons, He loves us.

Please, take some time on or around Christmas Day. Get out of your private agendas to celebrate the largest gift we receive on this planet—belonging!

A FAMILY CELEBRATION—IN TWO PARTS

I. *Gifts Seen! The family together with the gifts.*

Head of the Family: In the exchange of gifts, we as a family (and with our friends too) take part in an act of love. We sense that all of this has come from the ancient story of the Wise Men and their gifts to the Christ child.

Family: The gifts they gave were not to fulfill an obligation, but to respond to an event which they could not fully understand, but which they could symbolize.

Since gifts are symbols of love just as stoplights are symbols of traffic regulation, it may be good to stop here briefly to discuss the meaning of symbols, especially with younger children. Santa may also be an example to use.

Head of the Family: Our gifts to each other are therefore tokens and symbols of our love for each other,

Family: and also symbols of our appreciation to God for giving us each other.

Head of the Family: (as a prayer) Help us, O God, to know how to give and receive from each other. Make us sensitive to just how much we need each other.

Family: All through the year, O Lord, we look to each other for support and understanding. Let us now share that emotion and feeling with each other as we share the gifts.

Together: Amen.

Let the fun of exchanging gifts take place according to family custom. Then, either set a new time aside for II. Gifts

Unseen, *or begin right away by filling the Family Cup of Bless-*
ing and setting it in your midst.

II. *Gifts Unseen! A more quiet time, reflecting the theme*
of Christ's birth, and a time to share hopes and dreams.

Head of the Family: Today, O Lord, we give our Cup of
Blessing a new significance. In our own human history, You
have come in our flesh, born long ago in a crude barn.

Family: Our Cup, therefore, is a birthday Cup!

Head of the Family: And as it is shared by all, may it symbolize that historical event,

Family: and the Unseen Gift of Life in the person of Your
Son.

Head of the Family: As we receive Your Unseen Gifts again
this Christmas, Father, we see and know them as if in a dark
glass,

Family: for life has already become ours, yet its promises in
Christ go beyond the mere fact of our breathing.

Head of the Family: We have learned, in our freedom, to
depend, in hope, upon Your promises,

Family: and have touched the Unseen Gift from time to
time.

Head of the Family: We have felt the mystery of Your
Promises even though we have not been able to put these
feelings into words,

Family: and when we have dared to trust, we have experienced Life, and we are grateful.

Head of the Family: Christ is born!

Family: God cares!

Together: Amen!

The Cup of Blessing—The Christmas Cup—may be shared. Whatever words are used when the Cup is passed, let them be reflective, joyous, and simple—even "Happy birthday."

5. Celebrating The New Year

New Year's Eve sometimes finds the family going in different directions. New Year's Day is devoted, in the literal sense, to football, with the fresh new year getting but a few pat phrases said about it and the new numerals repeated quizzically until the ear gets used to them. It should get more attention—and family style too! New Year celebrations are rich in history and have invaded the religious world ever since man became aware of the passing of time.

A LITURGY FOR FAMILY AND FRIENDS

Leader: There is an awareness that we all acknowledge today, which goes beyond simply changing the number of the year.

All: We are aware of the passing of time.

Leader: But beyond the passing of time, however profound that may be for any of us, we are also sensitive to impulses our forefathers had at such momentous occasions.

Here may be read one of hundreds of stories concerning the way man has come to understand the new year.

One of the Old Testament themes out of the Holiness Code of Leviticus proclaims that, with the blowing of festal trumpets, the faithful should gather at the beginning of the new year to reaffirm their at-one-ment. The idea of reconciliation —the atonement—dominates the religious history of the Jews. Rosh Hashana, with "rosh" meaning "head of" and "ha-sha-na," "the year," precedes Yom Kippur, or the Day of Atonement. The well-known practice of making "resolutions" for the new year represents a popularization of the kind of faithful intent by the believer to prepare himself for certain acts of reconciliation within the community.

Leader: May we also become reflective and hope-full as we enter into a new year of opportunities.

Take time to identify those times and occasions when at-one-ment was evidenced in family, work, self, etc.

Leader: Remembering, with thanks, the times when certain people gave us needed support and the encouragement to be reconcilers ourselves, we now look to a new day filled with yet-to-be-lived hopes and dreams.

All: So we pass the Cup of Blessing to each other, not only as a sign of peace and love shared, but as an opportunity for each of us to share a hope, a plan, a dream.

Take time, each in turn as the Cup comes around, for this sharing in openness and trust.

Leader: (as a prayer) Give us Your Holy Spirit, O Father, in the days and months which lie ahead. Let us be open to changes.

All: Let us listen to each other,

Leader: And respond to new situations.

All: Let us be empathetic to those in search of human fulfillment,

Leader: And bring to them fresh options for their freedom. And let us always be bringers of peace to our troubled world.

A prayer to be prayed by all: To be a responsible person in the year ahead means that we must be responsive listeners. Father, teach us to listen to each other. Make us understand that this world of Yours does not always cry out in clear tones. Often our brother's needs become muted, and at other times they are couched in the blatant language of the man who sounds too sure of himself. Help us to approach this new year as reconcilers, as was Your Son Jesus Christ, and to act in love and patience toward all who may interrupt our coming days. Amen.

6. February's Heroes

It may be a bit more sensible to treat our historical figures either with a touch of humor or, at least, within the context of the tragedy which almost always surrounded their lives. Never should they be treated as out-and-out heroes in the popular meaning of that word!

Heroes have a way of standing apart from, or, as the saying goes, of "lording it over," their contemporaries, and certainly over us non-heroes!

But there is a certain loneliness about the so-called hero. Forgetting Hollywood glamor and fictionalized romantic portrayals of American historical personalities, we find their real lives touched with surprisingly unglamorous situations. There is often an indescribable kind of fervor, or call it passion or love, which motivates their lives. More often than not they themselves are, or at least would be, surprised at being called a hero. Unfortunately, February's birthday remembrances, including the natal days of Washington and Lincoln, have been popularized in bad school drama and greeting card myths which have filled the gaps of legalized memorials and days off from work. We all have a few uneasy feelings about our heroes, not because they failed to be great when greatness was needed, but because we have accidentally pushed and shoved their lives beyond the reaches of human sensitivity into that terrifyingly aloof category of Hero!

First: *Read something about the historical personality. Try to find a letter or two written by him or her. They reveal more than the historian's reflections.*

Then: *Read I Corinthians 13. This famous chapter is most interesting when the thoughts of human heroism are read between the lines.*

Finally: *A liturgy for all who have examined the dimensions of human genius, martyrdom, inventiveness, and who have wondered what passion, what love, might have been the motivating part of the life of those we so easily call heroes!*

A LITANY ON LOVE AND DEEDS

Leader: We may have the gifts of scientific prediction and understand the behavior of molecules; we may break into the storehouses of nature and bring forth new insights,

People: but devoid of love, all these mean nothing, O Lord.

Leader: We may give our goods to feed the poor; we may bestow gifts to charity,

People: but devoid of love, all these mean nothing, O Lord!

Leader: We may die the death of a martyr and spill our blood as a symbol of honor for generations unborn,

People: but devoid of love, all these mean nothing, O Lord!

Leader: O Father, we must come to see that a man may be self-centered in his self-denial and self-righteous in his self-sacrifice; our generosity may feed our ego and our piety our pride.

People: Without love, benevolence becomes egotism and martyrdom becomes spiritual pride.

Leader: But the greatest of all virtues is love!

People: In a world dependent upon force, coercive tyranny, and bloody violence, we are challenged by Your loving Son to follow His compassion,

Leader: and to discover that unarmed love is the most powerful force in the world.

People: Amen—so be it!

7. Valentine's Day

What a day for loving! Bring the Cup of Blessing to the dinner table and let it be used along with the exchange of the heart-shaped box of bonbons, appropriate Valentine cards, or what have you.

Leader: If we permit others to love us, then they make claims on our lives.

Family: We belong to them.

Leader: We know then that it is a difficult thing to be loved!

Family: Help us, Lord, to be loved as well as to love.

Leader: When we want to be free, those who love us tie us down.

Family: For such is the depth of love.

Leader: When we want to think of ourselves as being inadequate, those who love us make us feel greater than we are prepared to feel.

Family: For such is the depth of love.

Leader: When we want to be hard-nosed or angry, those who love us appeal to our sensitivity and ask us to be gentle.

Family: For such is the depth of love.

Leader: When we feel moody, those who love us ask us to come and play with them and to laugh.

Family: To be loved means to belong to others.

Leader: Teach us the mystery of being loved, O Lord, and help us to believe that those who say they love us really do; and allow us to believe that their love for us is real.

Family: Keep us from exploiting or manipulating each other out of the fear that we are not worthy of true love.

Leader: In the bleakness of February, we celebrate a day of love. Make each day in our lives a day of Good News.

Family: The Good News is the love of Jesus Christ.

All: Amen.

8. Mother's Day

Words for all but Mom: After the cards and presents have been given, let the Cup of Blessing be filled and the family gather. Giving God thanks for Mom is a tough job, especially for the children who want to say so much simply because Mother is so much a part of their growing years. And Dad's usual approach will want to be a bit less "mushy" than some of the cards he can buy, but still filled with deep love and the "right" word for the occasion.

Dad (or oldest child): Long ago, a mother whom we have all come to know as Mary, the mother of Jesus, spoke some very beautiful and meaningful words. The words she prayed were about her role as a mother and especially about her acceptance, in trust, of the responsibility God was to give her.

Oldest child (or Dad) then reads: *Luke 1:46-55. Either the new Jerusalem Bible or a similarly good translation is suggested.*

Dad (or oldest child): We give thanks to God that He has made new life come through human beings called mothers and fathers,

Family: and we give special thanks for Mom.

Dad (or oldest child): We know that we take her love for each of us for granted, but that is only because we know that we can trust it and depend upon it every day,

Family: and we are happy about that kind of love.

Dad (or oldest child): Today we remember those times and occasions when her love for us has been both special and the everyday-kind-of-love which none of us could think of doing without.

Let each member of the family remember the ordinary things Mom does, and the special times when her support, words, or whatever were "just right." Have fun with this part of the family liturgy.

Dad (or oldest child): Lord of us all, as we share the Cup of Blessing again today with special thanks for a special woman in our house, let us be mindful of how each member of our family does the "ordinary" kind of loving toward all the rest of us and of how wonderful it is to know love because of Family! Your grace has provided us with each other,

Family: and we are thankful.

Dad (or oldest child): Help each of us to keep on loving in the ordinary ways as well as the special ones.

Family: Make it so, Lord.

As you pass the Cup, and a kiss too, let Mom have a few moments to respond in her own way.

9. Father's Day

Father's Day can be very important in the sense that most of us—as children—grow up depending upon a God who goes by the name "Father." Those who minister to children who have experienced desertion by their biological father either through divorce or through death, often transfer their feelings to thoughts about God. What a responsibility we earthly fathers have, since we know that God is pictured by children as wearing our clothes and acting with our parental habits. (See section on book recommendations.) With this in mind, let us invite the whole family to recognize Dad in special ways!

Mother (or one of the children): We fill our Cup of Blessing today because we want to share thoughts and feelings about the love we have for someone very special in our family.

Children: We give our thanks to God for our father and for the love he gives us.

Mother: (as a prayer) Behind that word "father" there is so much that we already know about, trust in, hope for and sense,

Children: because we first came to know how right it was for fathers to love and for us to place our trust in them since we have learned to call You Father.

Mother: Father of us all, our God and our Lord, You have provided us with a hint of what it means to be accepted and loved whenever we as a family have come to know the security and trust of this family,

Children: and the example of complete trust which we have in the earthly father You have given us.

Mother: For us, father means (trust—*add the word which says it best for you and the children*).

Children: Grant to us all as a family, O Lord, that our trust in each other will come because we have learned to trust You as our Father.

You might conclude the family celebration with kisses all around, passing the Cup, and/or with the familiar Lord's Prayer.

10. Halloween

The interesting history of the celebration of the Eve of Allhallows might be fascinating research for the whole family. Although its origin is pagan and superstitious practices are beyond anything Christian, there is a celebrational mood and suggestions toward the use of festive imagination which transform it into a good time for the Christian family.

A few celebrational hints: *Since Halloween comes on the eve of the Church's remembrance of the saints of all time, take an evening off with the family and try to remember a few of the saints by name. Most of us have been taught to think of saints as having lived in a kind of Holy History. We all know about St. Luke, St. Matthew, etc., but we have made them untouchable and removed by time. We would encourage you, however, to celebrate their touchableness freshly. When the*

Church speaks of "Communion of Saints," it has been expansive enough to include men and women through history who have made an impact on the causes of joy, hope, peace, justice, and compassion and to do so in the name of Christ. Furthermore, the saints are usually controversial people. With such an understanding of the saints, we might include the names of Martin Luther King, Dag Hammarskjöld, and Dietrich Bonhoeffer as well as those of ancient days, such as Abraham, the man of hope, Amos, the bringer of justice, Francis of Assisi, and even a fellow by the name of St. Maximilian (c. 295 A.D., look him up).

Say a short prayer of thanks for their lives and the impressions they have made on us.

Pick a saint! Dress up, just for the fun of it, in a costume depicting the historical figure you choose to call "Saint." Fill the family Cup, and together with the family, toast the men and women who have punctuated the seeming inevitability of wars and conflicts with those times of joy and hope. Then give thanks for people who in history have healed and reconciled. Talk about them, dress up like them, and have fun.

A PRAYER

Either at the dinner table or in the family Halloween party:

Leader: Behind the idea of ghosts and goblins, we realize the opportunity to remember the real people who lived on our planet. We imagine how they must have sensed Your power and compassion, Father, and we rejoice at the response their lives made for good.

Family: We remember them tonight and give thanks to You, O God, for the lives of those who would risk love. Amen.

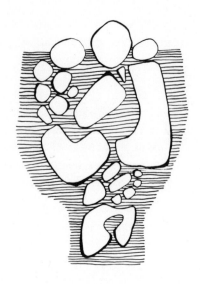

11. A Family Thanksgiving

This family service is not intended to be a substitute for the Thanksgiving Eve or Day worship at your church. Rather, it is intended as an enhancement and enlargement of family sensitivity to the whole theme of The Giving of Thanks!

Things to do: About a week or so before Thanksgiving, communicate with all those invited and suggest that they give thought concerning the possibility of each person offering a unique expression of his or her own thanks. A one-line prayer, a piece of home-made prose or poetry, or, for the more ambitious, a musical composition to sing around the piano or guitar! Don't be afraid to allow your emotions to show. And even though we have often made the giving of thanks into a very somber and superserious matter, remember that Christianity has usually been at its best whenever its thanksgiving was free, joyous, and loaded with the kind of trust which can relax.

For the imaginative: *Try to write the outline for what might turn into an impromptu Thanksgiving Day play. Using the ideas inherent within improvizational theater, you might identify the parts or roles you would like to see played by putting them on separate pieces of paper and handing them out either before Thanksgiving or right after dinner. Role-playing can be great fun! Make sure you set the stage for all the characters. Tell all present "where" the scene is, "when" it occurs, "why" they are all there, and "what" they might find themselves doing. Of course, they already know "who" they are because you have told them. Role-playing is for your living room and has no resemblance to grand opera or anything else, so why not let your imagination roam and—on the general subject of giving thanks—see what happens when the family comes for Thanksgiving Day this year.*

Around the table: *Hold hands for the prayer. And then say, all together, or with the host saying the words for you:*

A THANKSGIVING PRAYER

Lord God, we come to this table as a family and first we want to say our word of thanks for being just that! If we have sometimes taken each other for granted, forgive us. Yet we know that today is not a day for confessing our separation but for proclaiming our unity with You in many ways. As individuals we are thankful that, in the silence of those moments only You may share with us, we have a God of acceptance to turn to! And as any of us here are old enough to experience the rich gifts of making family a reality in our lives, we know also how You have become the Father of us all in so many ways.

The past year, Lord, is before us all at this moment for reflection. The time we have been given is Your gift called life! We may have misused some of it, while affirming the rich potential of the gift of days during other times. Hear us now, Lord, either in silence or verbally, as we all tell You, with thanks, of the year of Life You have allowed us to spend. (Here either silent prayer may be the order, or each in turn may say a simple "thank You, Lord, for. . . .")

Finally, give us the good sense this day, dear God, to know that our family is a community of persons, all of whom are accepted in love by You. In our living together through the various stages of our lives, we know that we can truly be needed by each other. We sense that families use a kind of everyday love that doesn't get the attention of the song writers who romanticize love. But we are still thankful to You that family love can be just like Your Good News, like a Presence felt: dependable and full of trust from day to day. Thank you, in Jesus' name. Amen.

III. Special Occasions

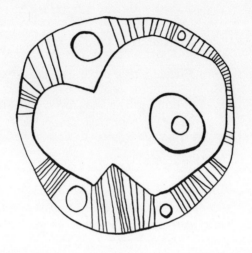

12. On the Birth of a Baby

Some starter words for the family: When things get quiet and the mood around the house tends to be reflective, gather the family around the Cup of Blessing and let the words of joy over the little miracle in your house flow! Include special friends and relatives, and your pastor as well as the other children in the family.

The New Father (with the Cup):
　　　　To my son (daughter)
　　　　　　a true gift from God
　　　A mystery from within us
　　　　　　and a person already shaped.

The New Mother (with the Cup):
    To flesh of my flesh
      carried with care
    Alive and free
      acceptable as God's child.

Pass the Cup of Blessing all around!

Now, before the family prayer, tell everyone the meaning behind the child's name. If your pastor is present, ask for his blessings and words, and let everyone share in words of hope and joy in an informal way.

Finally, and most important, the words of thanks to God —the expression of gratitude which a family feels at the birth of a child! Your own words, however simple, are the best words. Sometimes, however, you can't really express what your heart holds. The words which follow allow for only one theme to be touched upon: trust. Use them together as a family, in a circle of prayer, and reflect on the gift God has given you.

A FAMILY PRAYER OF TRUST

For all to pray

Father of us all
   teach us to trust
Let the lesson of the small gift of life
   which we claim to be ours
Be sufficient to remind us all
   of the plans and the promises
You hold out
   for us.

If our thanks is to be honest and good
   then it should be sensitive
To just how much You must trust us
   with the fragile gifts of creation.

And so our timid words of thanks
   already know of the grace which invites our trust
And which will also allow our own son (daughter) to grow
   into a trusting human being.
Amen—may it be so!

13. Adoption into the Family

The adoptive and the biological families are very much alike.
They both share love, experience pain, needs, and joys. The
chief difference—and one to be celebrated by those who adopt
—is that adoptions hardly ever happen by accident! The word
"choosing" may get overworked, but it will have to be stressed
here too as the reason for such celebration. So, share your
new joy with family, friends, pastor, and say "thank you" to
God for your dreams made real.

At the crib, or with the new baby and friends whom you
have invited:

New Father: With a great sense of awe over the mystery of
life itself, and a deep recognition of its frailty, we thank You
Lord for the trust You have given to us as parents.

New Mother: For this flesh-and-blood child whom we have named ———— we give You our humble thanks.

New Father: None of us are "born fathers" or "born mothers," and the loving and caring for a child comes as a fresh new surprise every day.

New Mother: So give us the grace to be open to those new days and to each other, that we may be, in the best sense, a family.

New Father: We thank You for ————.

New Mother: And for each other, and especially for ————. (*Here name other children already a part of the family.*)

If children are able to read or participate in welcoming the new baby, then encourage them to say a simple prayer of "thank you." It is important that all the children feel genuinely included.

Then raise the Cup of Blessing and share it, each sip to be followed by a wish for the newest gift from God.

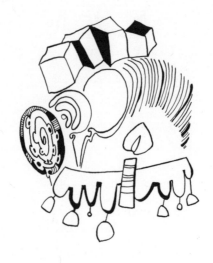

14· Celebration of a Birthday—Pre-Teen

The following may be used at a birthday party with friends or with the immediate family, depending upon circumstances. The leader may be one parent, an adult, relative, or a friend, as you choose.

Leader: It is with special joy and happiness that we all come together today to celebrate the birthday of ———. May we all give our thanks to God for this young life, and pray that he (she) will always know the greatness of His Gifts of Love.

Family: The love from God for ——— is the same love that we all want to show to each other.

Leader: We are glad that the gift of love has been a part of the life of ———. We are also glad that, as the years go by, we may all grow in our love and trust in each other.

Family: We thank You, Father in heaven, for ——— and for each other.

Or, if this liturgy is to be shared with friends:

Leader: It is with special joy that we call good friends together today. We are here to celebrate the birthday of ———. May we all give our thanks to God for this young life, and pray that he (she) will always know the greatness of His love.

Friends: The love from God for ——— is like the love we all try to show in our lives. We are glad that love for each other makes our friendship happy and able to grow.

Now, whether it be with family or friends, or both, let the Cup of Blessing be filled and shared.

Leader: The Cup of Blessing is special for our family. Today it is a birthday Cup for ———, and it means that we are one in God and the gift of His loving creation, our son (daughter).

A VERY SPECIAL TIME FOR WISHING

After the Cup has been passed, talk about the new year to come and of the privileges and responsibilities which lie ahead for someone a year older. It is good to let the birthday child suggest one new privilege he would like, and also, one new responsibility. Final decisions as to both may then be tempered by further family conversation.

It may also be revealing and provide the birthday celebrant with encouragement, either with friends or family (but especially with the family), to let everyone take a turn at expressing a wish for the birthday boy or girl for the year ahead.

15. Celebration of a Birthday—Teen

The following is most appropriate within the family. The leader may be a parent or someone else, depending upon circumstances.

Leader: We come together as a family to raise a special Cup of Blessing. We celebrate the birthday of ———. We give thanks to God for his (her) life and especially for these exciting and maturing years in which life-style directions and decisions are being sought out.

Family: Help us, O God, to recognize the importance of family trust and openness during our all-too-short years together. Help us achieve mutual willingness to listen to each other in love.

Leader: We are thankful for the expressions of trust and empathy which we have already known as a family,

Family: and for the moments of unspoken love we have shared together.

Leader: And for all of Your blessings, Father, especially the life of the one whose birthday we enjoy together today, we give thanks.

Family: Guide and love us all, for we pray in Christ's Name. Amen.

The birthday celebrant may wish to respond.

Let the Cup of Blessing be filled. Let it represent the oneness of the family's love. It may be appropriate to talk about new privileges and new responsibilities now that he (she) is a year older. And, in so far as maturity of the emotional variety is evidenced on the part of all, allow the decisions to be made by the birthday celebrant.

Let each member of the family make a wish for the birthday boy or girl for the year ahead. Share the wishes openly, with joy, and help each other seek out ways to make the wishes come true. Have a good family day!

16. Birthday of an Adult

The following may be used with family or among friends. The leader may be a member of the family (older child or spouse), or a good friend.

Leader: With special joy we come to celebrate ———'s birthday today. May the blessings of God flow in his (her) life.

Family: We are thankful for the life and spirit of the one whose birthday we celebrate.

Leader: May he (she) always be free in Christ.

Family: May it ever be so.

The birthday celebrant may want to respond with particular words of thanks to family and friends, or with a brief prayer of thanks to God for all the blessings of life.

Fill the Cup of Blessing and let it represent the oneness of the family's love. Though new privileges and responsibilities are usually not considered a part of the birthday of an adult, it may still be interesting to engage in family conversation about such matters, especially in terms of family growth.

Let each member of the family make a wish for the celebrant for the year ahead. Share the wishes openly, and, in joy and anticipation, help each other seek out ways to make the wishes come true.

17. A Baptismal Birthday Celebration

It is suggested that the members of your family choose a particular day of the year to represent the "Baptismal Day" for every member of the family. A cake or other festive cooking is very much in order. Let the day be both festive and reflective. Talk together about those "Unseen Gifts" of the Spirit received by each in the family over the past year. Then there are hopes and expectations for the year to come, especially because your family has identified itself, one by one in Baptism, with the special plan and will of Jesus Christ. So, instead of exchanging gifts you can see, exchange the gifts of the Spirit: felt, known, but rarely put into words! Today, do it!

The Cup of Blessing may be filled, along with the cake or . . .

Leader: As our Cup of Blessing is raised today, we all pause to remember that when we were Baptized, we each were blessed with the Gift of New Life.

Family: *A time for remembering—when, where, how, names of those involved in the Baptism—and for sharing words about the fact that a lovely mystery has become the common experience of everyone in the home.*

Leader: We are thankful for our memories and for the acknowledgment of the community of humans known as the Church who share the trust as well as the grace which has become ours.

Family: Help us live each day with confidence, O Lord.

Leader: Each of us has received a birthday in Christ, being buried with Him in the symbolic water and raised with Him in the hope of Life without end.

Family: Help us live each day with renewed faith, O Lord.

The family may now share the Cup and all else around the table. As the Cup is shared, you may use special words to each other, words which are hints concerning the mystery of the gift of Baptism; i.e., "I wish you . . . love . . . peace . . . hope . . . joy . . . insight . . . empathy. You may want to sing, pray a spontaneous prayer of thanks, or just talk as a family as you conclude the celebration. But let it all be done with the joy which shows that you are truly on the receiving end of the greatest gift in the world!

18. Recognition of Advancement

There are times when someone in the family is cited for making a contribution to life, when children go to a new grade, when Dad (or Mom) receives a degree, when an unexpected raise or promotion is announced. Then, bring out the Cup of Blessing and fill it with your favorite juice and share the happiness together.

A Chosen Member of the Family: Advancement means joy! So let us celebrate with real thanks to God. *Pour the liquid and share it with words of congratulations, of personal happiness, etc. Then make the Cup ready for a second sharing.* Advancement means the anguish of newness! Let us now celebrate new possibilities.

Speak together about the implications of the advance, hopes, yet-to-be-fulfilled plans, etc.

51

A PRAYER OF THANKS

By a person who would speak for all.

Being responsible, O God, is not the easiest thing in life. When any of us receive congratulations and the applause of others, we tend to respond with mixed emotions. All of the efforts of past days now seem well spent, and we sense that being responsible was indeed worthwhile. At the same time, in our deepest reflections, even the smallest spotlight of attention may cause us to have the common human problem of an enlarged view of ourselves. Keep us sane when others tell us "well done." And at the same time, encourage us to seek out the words of the One who was Servant of us all, who said, "Well done, good and faithful servant"; in Christ. Amen.

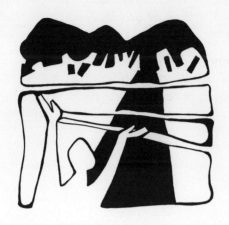

19. Celebration of a Homecoming

In a day of great mobility it is not uncommon for members of the family to be away from home from time to time. This little liturgy has the family communicate in some special ways within the framework of a homecoming celebration.

The Cup of Blessing may be filled at some convenient time after dinner, or whenever it seems relaxing for the whole family. Let there be one chosen member of the family pray the following prayer:

PRAYER

Dear Father, we pass our Cup of Blessing with real understanding of what it means to be together and to share with each other the blessings of the family. We all seem to increase the number of our daily problems when we're apart. Teach us always to be grateful to You for each other's lives. Amen.

Any amount of deliberately dedicated family time, whether it be time to tell about the things that happened while apart from each other, or to share new plans, etc., is especially good after coming home from a number of days separated from loved ones.

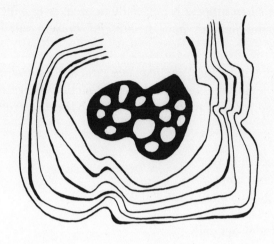

20. Celebration of a Wedding Anniversary

This short liturgy is for husband and wife to share. The family together may use the "Liturgy for the Family at Home."

Who knows what married couples speak of, dream of, argue over, and hold in reserve as the hidden agenda for rare moments. We would not be so bold as to shape words which, in a very real sense, ought to be the free, intimate, and mutually understood vocabulary of a married couple. The only item even remotely liturgical on this page is the Lord's Prayer. We would suggest, however, that some time be set aside to talk about the lives you lead together, the destiny under God which you share together, the children which might be yours as a part of God's grace, the words you use "at" or "for" each other, the times when support is especially needed, or at least to pray together the familiar and meaningful prayer which Christ taught.

We all "make love" in marriage; not only physically, but with our emotions, our words, our touching of each other. Praise God for the lavish dimensions of Making Love!

So be it!

Our Father in heaven
holy be Your name.
Your kingdom come, Your will be done,
on earth as in heaven.
Give us today our daily bread.
Forgive us our sins
as we forgive those who sin against us.
Save us in the time of trial,
and deliver us from evil,
For Yours is the kingdom, the power, and the glory,
Forever, Amen.

21. Welcoming an Overnight Guest

Sometimes there are "the greatest" of people who come to stay with your family for a time and you want to let them in on the fact that your love for them is rooted in Christ. Often this is difficult to say without having it burst out in accidentally stilted words in the "grace" before the meal. This liturgy is an attempt to open up even brief conversation at the dinner table concerning the meanings of deeper relationships.

Take the Cup of Blessing and explain to your guests what it means to the family and how you use it from time to time. Let them know that the family Cup is now to be enlarged simply because you want to include your guests in love.

Fill the Cup and offer a brief prayer, or, if more appropriate, a toast to friendship and a pledge of the family's love and affection.

Let the conversation flow freely.

22. Welcoming New Neighbors

Most neighborhoods are very "come-and-go" kinds of places. So, welcoming new neighbors may be a pretty essential act lest communication with the folks who live around you either exists on minimal levels or, as in many cases, never really gets started.

Children have a difficult emotional time moving into a new neighborhood. If their moodiness shows a reluctance to meet "new kids," it is only because the loss of good pals back home has, at every age, been a powerful factor. At any rate, moving is always an emotional strain as well as a backache producer. We all know there is a lot about neighbor-love in the New Testament and we also realize that you don't usually get to plan your neighborhood. People just move in! All kinds, sizes, shapes, colors! And isn't that great? Accept them all as gifts of Grace. Let the whole family be open to the lives of others, to learn from them and to be understanding of their family life styles.

No opening up of the family celebration book will do when you go to meet the new neighbors or invite them over. (Might they not wonder about your motives or maybe even think you are trying to "evangelize" them? They might interpret your "religious" language to be a sophisticated con job on behalf of the local church.) So, when they are visiting you, simply get the Family Cup of Blessing out and share a bit of the grape or another appropriate juice for all family seasons. Let it be a token—a sip shared all around—along with a fit word concerning your family's sincere welcome to the neighborhood. Make it a happy bon mot. Who knows, you might be welcoming the future in-laws!

23 Children's Liturgy for Making up Again

This little liturgy may be used by friends or brothers and sisters who, as sometimes happens, fight with each other.

First Child: Dear God, we want to say that we are sorry for becoming angry (selfish, stubborn, nasty) with each other.

Second Child: We ask forgiveness from each other and ask you to help us love each other. Amen.

Parent or oldest in family may then take the Cup of Blessing, fill it, and pass it around with appropriate words, such as, "This is for making up."

24 Liturgy for the Family at Home

Sometimes the family simply wants to "stay home" and spend time enjoying each other as well as the blessings of family routine in familiar surroundings. This liturgy celebrates that time.

Leader: For human life; for the skills and imagination which make beautiful things, and for the joy of the shelter we call our home:

Family: We give thanks, O Lord.

Leader: For marriage and family; for the mystery and joy of flesh made one; for family forgiveness and burdens as well as hopes shared; for secrets kept in love; for being amused with and by each other, and for all our family holds in common:

Family: We give thanks, O Lord.

Leader: For our children and for their energy and curiosity; for brave play and good frankness; for their sudden sympathies and their irreverence toward worn-out values; for their search for freedom and their solemn vows:

Family: We give thanks, O Lord.

Leader: For growing up and out of houses which grow old, for entering different places of brick and mortar; for this place we call home:

Family: We ask your blessing, O Lord.

Leader: Give us not only the freedom to celebrate our individuality but also the sense to know how we are a family; and especially, at this moment, give us a deep appreciation of the love which binds us as one:

Family: Thank you, Father, for being present. Amen.

25. First Communion

This is for that grace-filled day when the commonness of bread and the fresh taste of the fruit of the vine become invested with meaning beyond words! It is at your child's First Communion that the joy of discovering new supportiveness within the family may be shared. Make a full-fledged party of the occasion. Invite the pastor, friends, and family. Then, with all gathered around the table, share together your happiness and sense of new grace and responsibilities.

AT THE FAMILY TABLE

Head of the Family: First Communion is rarely, if ever, thought of as simply gaining a privilege because of what can be demonstrated, memorized, performed, or considered as an act of human accomplishment. Quite the opposite is true!

Though responsibility to our fellow man is sharpened, the central idea behind the Holy Communion is that God Himself acts toward us with His own grace in a manner quite apart from any merit, humanly speaking. For us simply to know that this really happens to us is enough! If there were ever a time for simply "being loved," this is it.

Take the Cup of Blessing and let the one who is the family host make the first "toast" to the new communicant. When all around the table have offered words of congratulations and hope, allow the First Communion boy or girl to respond in his or her own way. Let it be a happy time, concluding with this or another prayer of your choice.

The Prayer: It is Your accepting grace and Your unmatched compassion which we celebrate today, O Lord. The Body and the Blood of Your Son is meant to touch our bodies and lives too. He has indeed come in our history and he continues to strengthen and support us in the forgiving love of the Supper he instituted. Help us to be always thankful that Your willingness to love our fragile humanity has allowed You to shape Your love in the Servant Lord who gave Himself for us. Make us all especially aware that, as we receive Your gift, You do not offer us reasons, but love. We pray with thank-filled hearts for ———— and gratefully receive him (her) into the circle of those who dare to let You love Your creation; in Jesus' name. Amen.

26. An Engagement in the Family

Those who are engaged to be married have secrets from the rest of us. Of course! But the rest of us also want to be supportive and somehow to share that rare joy. So, this celebration is for the family (or families) of the engaged couple; hopefully, along with the couple to be married.

A hint to the in-laws: *An appropriate engagement gift, and something which you can surely use in this celebration, is a Cup of Blessing. (See the Foreword for the history of the Cup itself.) The Bride and Groom to-be may also enjoy helping you pick out a Cup to symbolize a new union and a fresh love.*

A symbol within the marriage service: *Some of the marriage services now include the symbolism of the shared Cup, not as a substitute for the Holy Communion, but as a sign of the marriage itself. It might be something you wish to discuss with the officiating pastor.*

A healthy by-product of the Engagement Celebration: *Can either of the families know and like each other that well by this time? Let the shared Cup invite festivity and good family fun.*

A LITURGY FOR THE OCCASION

Leader: The joy we all share today is a happiness born out of love.

Family: The Cup we offer as our gift is a symbol of that same love.

Leader: May this young couple know the depth of give-and-take within their love.

Family: May the Cup be a sign of their willingness not only to be lovers, but also to be recipients of the love from God by which they are continually loved.

THE FAMILY PRAYER

All: Dear God, we pray today in the Name of Your Son who knew the joys of weddings and the anxieties of families as He turned the water at Cana into the "best wine." As we fill our Cup, we praise You and thank You for an unfickle love and ask that it be bestowed upon the new and fragile compassion within our families. Be with them and call them to trust, always. Amen.

Finally: *Make a wish for the couple! Go around the room, person by person, including the children. Share wishes and hopes for the bride and groom to-be. Then open the rest of the fruit of the grape and let the evening flow on!*

Praise Him. We have a God of love!

27. A Celebration On Vacation

Some starter words for the family: If you can, find the right "setting" for reflections on being together at a time and in a place other than that associated with routine. If there is natural beauty around you, include it and let it help you each to find the "natural" beauty in each other as well as in God. Use a vacation cup for the shared blessing and take along the family Bible for the reading everyone has time for on vacation. Relax! Time out from work is no sin! Remember, at least one interpretation says that work—not rest—is the reward for sin. Thank God for vacation!

Fill the Cup of Blessing, and with the family gathered, say:

Head of the Family: For time off from responsibilities and for the luxury of having certain days made free for each other,

Family: we give thanks.

Head of the Family: For this new day and for the re-creation of body, minds, spirit, and emotion,

Family: we give thanks.

Head of the Family: For knowing that the freedom to say to each other that we have "nothing to do" comes not from despair but from joyous anticipation.

Family: we give thanks.

Head of the Family: For time to listen: to nature, to trees and wind and voices and the sounds of Your wondrous creation,

Family: we give thanks.

Head of the Family: For time to touch each other, and to accept ourselves, and for understanding once again our dependency upon each other and on You,

Family: we give thanks.

Head of the Family: Finally, for our family and for whatever we have already allowed ourselves to become to each other: need and needing, lifted and lifting, loved and loving,

Family: grant us an awareness of Your creation all around us, and especially the creation we have come to know as our family. Amen.

Besides the many Psalms and favorite readings you might have, it is suggested that you read Matthew 6:19-34. Pick an easy-to-read version and let the deep truths of Christ's words sink way in.

28. Discovery of Pregnancy

Whenever two lives have met in the depth of love and the surprise is "I'm going to have a baby," there are few adjectives to describe the moment!

Husband and wife together: An act of love was
and now is
and will become
by a Grace beyond us!

A prayer for discovery time (*And for the intervening days which lead to the miracle itself!*): Say it together:

O God, we feel the gift of life,
a secret made to be ours
and we are grateful.

May Your love for us and Your
    trust in our impending parenthood
    be noted this day by us both.
We humbly accept Your grace.
    Make us sensitive to Your gift. Amen.

For the family with young children who may be excited about getting a new brother or sister, there may be those wonderful moments when they will want to put tender and careful hands on Mommy's tummy to feel the miracle of new life. A prayer for and with them is also in order. Here is one youngsters will understand.

By one or both of the parents: O God, we give thanks as a family for a new baby growing this very minute inside of Mommy. Even though we cannot explain the mystery and wonder of it all, we know that You are giving our family the gift of new life because You love not only us but also everyone and everything You make. Help us love the new baby, too. We pray in the name of Your Son. Amen.

29. Before Entering the Hospital

Who among us goes to the hospital as a patient without even a smidgen of anxiety? Hospitals are white and antiseptic and never-private-enough kinds of places.

This little liturgy is for the family as well as for the one to be hospitalized and, if you like, sharable with your pastor or understanding neighbors.

First: *Take a few relaxing moments together as a family to talk about your feelings concerning the upcoming stay in the hospital. Even with a small bag packed, children will want to raise all kinds of questions which may be too complicated for them to state. They know it will be no typical vacation-fun trip, and they probably want to hear some words from some-one which will give them a view of what will be happening over the next days or weeks. Don't evade their questions, even the ones felt but not articulated. Children have anxieties only when they are denied their share in the fears as well as the hopes and dreams of the family itself.*

A prayer with the family together: God of us all, if we seem better able to get ready for the hospital in physical ways than we do emotionally, forgive us. We cannot seem to get over the mystery of our own body and all of its complications. We know that our inner parts are balanced delicately and that hospitalization is sometimes required. It is hard to talk about, however, even when we reach into the deepest part of who we are together as family. But we pray that you will keep each of us from having unnecessary and irrational fears. Remind us that You have already provided each of us with a natural healing process more astounding than the compassionate treatment given in the hospital. Encourage us in hope and attend us all with Your love and Your grace. Amen.

30. On the Death of a Pet

Nearly every one of our homes, at some time during the growing-up period of our children, welcomes a funny-looking mutt, cat, bird, guinea pig, or bowl full of treasured guppies. They, like all of us, die, and there is sadness on the part of us all. Here are a few helps for that occasion.

Gather the family together.

Leader: Because of the sadness we all feel today at ————'s death, we ought to talk about what this pet has meant to us.

Even though we all are aware that pets may be treated by some children as if they were human, there is undoubtedly an emotional loss, and just a simple invitation by a parent to sit down and talk about the pet can mean a great deal to young children. You'll be expressing care through the time taken.

Leader: Let's take this time to read from Scripture about the meaning of death and the hope that we might have for all of God's creatures, including the animals and the birds and the fish.

Appoint someone to read Psalm 148.

Leader: It is good for us all to be reminded that God's love covers everything He ever made.

Family: We are thankful for the life of our own pet ——— and we know that our sadness at its death can be turned into joy and hope because of God's love for His creation.

Another reading, this time from the New Testament, might be from I Corinthians 15.

Leader: We take our Family Cup of Blessing and share it today because we also know that it symbolizes the Gift of Love from God, the Love by which we are all loved!

Family: Thank You, Father, for the Gift of Life, now and beyond our death. Amen.

P.S. to parents: If the conversation gets around to the question of a pet heaven, I hope you will not discourage it. We can all be purists, I suppose, about such things. But let's not. It always amazes me that somehow the scope of God's intentions about us earthlings outstrips my fantasies. Children's dreams and fantasies may be refreshing hints about the grace of God, and may just help a lot of us parents out of adult ruts.

31. Preparation for a Funeral

Helping children accept the fact that people—favorite people in particular—die is a problem for most families. This little liturgy is meant for such a time. It is also meant as a catharsis for the whole family, especially when there seems to be indication that the days ahead will be particularly difficult or where a lengthy wake might become an emotional drain on the whole family.

To be read by a member of the family: Our family faces that which comes to everyone, the death of someone we love. (*Name the person who has died*) has lived and touched our family. We must now realize, however, that we are the ones left with pain and loss at his (her) death. In that sense, God has given us tears. Tears replace words that won't come, and so we have no shame at all in helping each other release this emotion.

But there is another emotion—a kind of haunting affirmation—which is a part of our family understanding even now as we prepare for a funeral. It is the Resurrection! Even as we say the word, it sounds nearly unbelievable. Of course! The Gift of Life and the Resurrection are huge affronts to the so-called fact of death. Like the release of big red, yellow, and green balloons, they are a kind of counterpoint to our very real cry of loneliness. Help us know in truth and in hope, O God.

Before the family attends the wake or funeral: How shall our family accept the death of someone dearly loved? Not easily or with stifled emotions. Maybe funeral services should be much more hope-filled than they sometimes are and should celebrate, in the deepest sense of that word, the remembrances of a life which exchanged love for love, hope for hope. We therefore take time with the family to give thanks for the one who has died by remembering those times.

Such a time, however short it may be, will undoubtedly help the children. Many children see death as God's way of punishing man for something. Maybe as the family talks, such fears and misunderstandings may be corrected by caring parents.

A Prayer: Dear God, attend our family today and in the days ahead. We need to remember the miracle of Easter. As we face the death of someone we love, the whole idea of the resurrection becomes something more than a springtime event or a time-worn doctrine. You have given us the Gift of Life and we are grateful beyond words. Help each of us, at needful times during the period of mourning, to uphold those whose joy has turned to sorrow, to remember Your promises. In Christ, the Risen Lord, we pray. Amen.

IV. Seasonal Recognition

32. Celebration of Springtime

On or about March 21 the family may want to take note of the fact that we are all caught up in an "eternal return," season upon season! Spring, of all the four seasons, is possibly most remarkable. Out of seemingly nothing, there is new creation. This liturgy is for the time of New Birth in God's nature. Pick a place where spring is "best" and take the Bible along. Be prepared to dream a bit too.

THE DREAMS AND REFLECTIONS OF SPRINGTIME

First, read Song of Songs 2:10-13. *Make sure you have a clear and readable translation.*

Head of the Family: What does it mean to enter into a new season?

Family: What new birth and freshness is before us today?

Head of the Family: We acknowledge spring not only as a lengthening of days (as in lengthen or Lent) but as a time of resurrection.

Family: Help us to see, O God, what new Life surrounds us this day.

Take some time for musing, listening to the sounds of spring, and just being human and perceptive about the Gift of Life.

A SPRINGTIME PRAYER

O God, who gives life a certain poetry of light in the springtime, and who provides us with days longer and more sun, as well as days which seem shorter because of joys too quickly spent to savor, teach us to love the spring.

O God, who makes the time of newness return and still the return of it all is not a mere repetition of last year, and the feel of it is crowded with things yet to be done, teach us to love the spring.

Give us pause this day, with thanks, for the resurrection of Your Son, of the sun, of fresh mornings, of dreams and plans, of the touch of the greening earth and of the fresh Yes! You seem to be saying to everyone. Amen.

33. Celebration of Summertime

On or about June 22 let the family celebrate the gift of summer, with all of its glorious warmth and glimmer. It is a relaxing time usually, when man relates to earth more empathetically than at any other season of the year. It is good to know the God who creates so magnificently. That's what this family liturgy is all about!

THE DREAMS AND REFLECTIONS OF SUMMERTIME

First, read Psalm 104.

Head of the Family: What does it mean to enter a new season?

Family: What are summer's new creations? The crawling and buzzing things which retain the balance of life itself!

Head of the Family: What do our own plans and adventures include because of summer's invitation?

Family: What "time off" is available to us all to linger in full days and sunny evenings?

Take time for musing, listening to the sounds of summer, and just being human and perceptive about the Gift of Life.

A SUMMERTIME PRAYER

O God, who gives life a reprieve from the dark and provides us all with a time for re-creation, and of fullness to everything that lives and breathes, teach us to love the summer.

O God, who calls us away seasonally to learn to listen and smell and see all over again, and who makes us sensitive to the promise of life in Christ, teach us to love the summer.

Give us pause this day, with thanks, for the gifts of summer's fullness; of greens and yellows and pale blues, of laughing people and beautiful flowers, of intense thirst and cooling evenings, of being hot and tired, and of the resounding Life-affirming Yes! You seem to be saying to everyone. Amen.

34. Celebration of Autumn

On or about September 23 the family may want to take into account the seasonal changes, and accompanying emotional changes, going on around them. Autumn has its own mystique and seems to call out for us to realize that a new set of changes make for new opportunities. Take the family in hand and let the words of Scripture and musing as well as reflective prayer bring you into the season of autumn.

THE DREAMS AND REFLECTIONS OF AUTUMN

First, read Ecclesiastes 3:1-8.

Head of the Family: What does it mean to enter into a season often called "fall"?

Family: What new thoughts about time do we have as the days grow shorter?

Head of the Family: What do the shadows and falling snows and winds do to the mind?

Family: What sense of finiteness do we perceive?

Take time for musing, listening to the sounds of autumn, and just being human and perceptive about the Gift of Life.

AN AUTUMN PRAYER

O God, who paints the earth in purple vines and orange stalks and gives us times for games and thanksgivings, and who makes us quite sensitive to the shortness of each of our days,

teach us to love the autumn.

O God, who makes all things new, including the quick and dead, and who in due season gives meat to all living things, and provides us with hope and promises of Life yet to come,

teach us to love the autumn.

Give us pause this day, with thanks, for all that we perceive; in the freedom we have to die, the freedom to live before we die, the Good News that birth of fresh trust in You can come in the midst of our living. Amen.

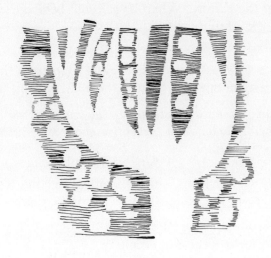

35. Celebration of Wintertime

On or about December 22 invite the family to celebrate the seasonal change within the context of Christmas just a few days away. Wintertime has its own way of beckoning the family to gather with a feeling of mutual dependence and trust. Let the liturgy which follows raise the level of that "family time" together.

THE DREAMS AND REFLECTIONS OF WINTERTIME

First, read Luke 1:26-35 or Romans 8:22-25.

Head of the Family: What does it mean to enter into a new quarter of the year?

Family: What is there to be born for us in such darkness?

Head of the Family: What life calls out behind the barren trees and the white snow?

Family: What pulse is felt as the evergreen is decorated and we are again asked to wait upon our God and the plans He may have for our own birth in the midst of our life?

Take time for musing, listening to the sounds of wintertime, and just being human and perceptive about the Gift of Life.

A WINTERTIME PRAYER

O God, who gives us winter's waiting and the season of giving and receiving, and a time for putting our arms around each other,

teach us to love the wintertime.

O God, who in the cold of winter comes to speak to us as a helpless Infant yet still makes us understand that this Child has come to feel what we feel and in the process teach us about Your full acceptance,

teach us to love the wintertime.

Give us pause this day, with thanks, for the season when you became small for us, and of the times of love shared, of receiving a gift without embarrassment, and of knowing of the only gift which comes to touch the nakedness and the cold felt by all men from time to time: the Gift of Your Son, our Reconciler, Jesus Christ. Amen.

V. The Holy Supper

36. The Meal of Joyous Thanks

This family service is different from all the rest; it is the Lord's Supper set in the framework of the home, the very place of its origin. Because the Holy Communion is of such high value as reconciling act, and also because it calls us all to remember the "Host" as Jesus Christ, the Church has been careful to invite us to a Banquet of larger dimensions. This liturgy, then, is for the rare occasion when, upon your invitation, your own pastor, along with other invited guests, may come to participate in the Supper in the free, open, and sharing atmosphere of God's smallest of congregations: the home.

Have a "talk through" session with your own pastor and allow to enter into this liturgy those additional words and acts which you both deem appropriate.

Pre-Communion time: *Let the conversation be relaxed, informal, and festive. Remember that one of the oldest words for the Supper is Eucharist, which means Joyous Thanksgiving. If children are present, let them join in with questions. If they do not commune as yet, offer a blessing to each of them at the table. Know each other by name.*

At the table: *The host or hostess may wish to bring a short table prayer, as one would before a family meal. Husbands and wives may want to sit next to each other, especially because of the family dimension and meaning in the passing of the Cup. The Server (your pastor) may sit in the middle. The table may resemble the altar of your church as it is set for communion, or may simply hold candles, a chalice, or your Family Cup of Blessing, a bottle of the fruit of the vine and a loaf of bread.*

THE COMMUNION

Server: The Lord be with you.

Family: And with you too!

Server: Let us thank God for our fellowship in His Name.

Family: And let us call upon His Holy Spirit to be in our midst.

Server: Lord, our hearts rejoice in the oneness we perceive in You. Still, by Your Spirit tonight, give us the grace of new beginnings, of brokenness restored, of fresh patterns of trust, that Your Church might be witnessed in this room.

Family: Amen—so be it!

Server holds up the bread and then the Cup of Blessing with the following words:

Server: In the breaking of bread we see Your broken body given for us. In the drinking of the Cup we sense the mystery of blood shed for an alienated world of Your children.

Family: And for us it also means the joy of Your pardon, the birth of new hope, the bliss of Life itself, and the peace which passes understanding.

Server: So lift up your hearts.

Family: We lift them up to God.

Server: It is good and right to thank Him.

Family: Holy, Holy, Holy, Lord God of all power! Everything, everywhere, is filled with Your presence.

THE PRAYERS *by the family*

Prayer requests may now be made and shared all around the table; i.e., "for those not present," "for the renewal of the whole church," "for the joy of a baby born to . . ." You may use the phrase: Let us call upon the Lord for . . . Silent prayer or verbal expressions are both appropriate. The Server may conclude the intercessions and petitions.

THE MEAL OF JOYOUS THANKS

Server: Let us remember how Christ has made our communion together possible.

Family: "On the night when He was betrayed"

Server: He came to be like us that we might be more like Him

Family: "He took bread"

Server: He came to share our life that we might come to share in the very life of God

Family: "And when He had given thanks"

Server: We come to see the real Christ in the Supper: His forgetfulness of self as against our self-centeredness, His humility against our foolish pride, His trust against our fears and doubts.

Family: "He broke it, and gave it"

Server: For God so loved this world that He gave it His only Son

Family: "He gave it to His disciples"

Server: For He said to us, unless you turn and become as little children, you will not enter the kingdom of heaven.

Family: "He said, Take, eat"

Server: And along with the very bread, take forgiveness of each other as the very miracle itself. It is a gift!

Family: "Take and eat, for this is my body"

Server: The body which Joseph took, and was wrapped in a clean linen cloth, and laid in a new tomb.

Family: "My body, which is given for you"

Server: Who, in the flesh, told us that if we ask anything in His Name, He will do it!

Family: "Do this in remembrance of Me"

Server: We shall not be left desolate. He will come to us. Because He lives, we will live also.

Family: "After the same manner also He took the Cup"

Server: The Cup He drinks we will drink; and with the Baptism with which He is baptized, we will be baptized.

Family: "And when He had His supper and had given thanks, He gave it to them saying, Drink it, all of you"

Server: Then I saw a New Heaven and a New Earth; and I saw a Holy City, New Jerusalem. And I heard a great voice from the throne saying, Behold, the dwelling of God is with men. He will dwell with them, and they shall be His people, and God Himself will be with them. . . . Behold, I make all things new.

Family: "It is shed for you and for many"

Server: So judge not unless you want to be judged; God is love, and His love redeems and frees.

Family: "For the forgiveness of sins"

Server: The deathly results of sin are well known, but the free Gift from God is Life for All Time in Christ

Family: "Do this, then, as often as you drink it, remembering Me"

Server: May it ever be so.

Family: Amen, amen.

The bread may then be passed around the table with each person taking a piece. Then the Cup may be passed. Appropriate words may be: (for the bread) "This is the Body of Christ," and (for the Cup) "This is for our reconciliation."

THE THANKSGIVING

All may pray together: O God, our true home for each of the generations of man: look with Your grace upon this home and the families around this table; give husbands and wives both courage and joy to work at their love for each other; give parents and children more feelings than reasons for listening to each other, and make of each of our homes symbols of rest, support, compassion, and refreshment, and even a foretaste of our everlasting home in You; through Jesus Christ our Lord. Amen.

Other prayers which seem right for the occasion may then be prayed.

THE BENEDICTION *by the Server:*

Now to Him who is able to keep us from falling and to present us without blemish before the Presence of His glory with rejoicing, to the only God, our Savior through Jesus Christ our Lord, be glory, majesty, dominion, and authority, before all time and now and forever.

Family: Amen.

Fellowship over filled "cups of blessing" may now be enjoyed by all through the balance of the evening.

Some Books for and about the Family

The list of recommended books for and about the family could be nearly endless. I have found, however, that readers take quite seriously a short, handy list of solid, to-the-point books. In that light, here is my personal list, along with a few comments. I hope that you buy a few of them for your family. I know that you will enjoy them.

Eric Erickson, *Childhood and Society*. The core is in chapter 7 under the title of "The Eight Ages of Man" and what Erickson does to enhance your appreciation of the Trust theme in family life.

Eric Fromm, *The Art of Loving*. This author, like the one above, deals with empathy, and Fromm's little book has become a kind of classic.

Paul Tournier, *Secrets*. This thin book fairly bursts with insights into how our children grow up. Tournier's style is captivating.

Robert F. Capon, *The Supper of the Lamb*. An Episcopal priest writes a theologically peppered cookbook. It is sheer delight! You'll find yourself quoting his wild "toasts" at the dinner table.

Martin E. Marty, *Righteous Empire*. A witty, readable invitation to the Protestant to come to terms with how he got that way! If you like history which touches home base and provides reflection on current life styles, get this book.

Harvey Cox, *The Feast of Fools*. Cox invites—in our case the family—to rediscover both fantasy and festivity. If you like to depend upon tradition and Christian heritage, then let Cox help free it all up! It's a beautiful book full of surprises for today's Christian.

71 72 73 10 9 8 7 6 5 4 3 2 1